places I love come back to me like music

–sara teasdale

EARTH
SONG

a nature poems experience

s a r a   b a r k a t ,   e d i t o r

T. S. Poetry Press • New York

T. S. Poetry Press
New York
Tspoetry.com

Cover image by L.L. Barkat. llbarkat.com

ISBN 978-1-943120-60-4

Barkat, Sara

[Poetry. Nature. Ecopoetry.]

Earth Song: A Nature Poems Experience
    Sara Barkat, Editor

Table of Contents

From the Editor

My experience of nature started as a child, playing for hours with my friends in the woods behind our church. We called it The Great Ravine, because there was a ravine, and it led down to a little trickle of a marsh that was mostly mud, and if you climbed up the other side, a collection of small bushes and trees all tangled with vines. It wasn't, by any means, untouched, sitting as it was between buildings, houses, and a road—but it was undeniably *wild*. There's something, perhaps a kind of heart-feeling, that recognizes the difference between what's planned and what's wild, and there is something more terrifying and freeing in coming to face with true wildness, even for a moment, than any number of days spent wandering parks (as lovely as that also is).

That is where I started. And, years after I pored over the "How to Make a Green Club" page in the back of a DK encyclopedia, having gone through both hopeful work toward *reduce, reuse, recycle* as a child, when I knew that we could fix everything if we only tried hard enough; and hopelessness, faced in college with an Environmental Justice course that with its unrelenting "it's never enough" depressed me enough I quit the class—I find that reality only becomes more complicated, and the world more fraught.

But that's not the whole story. The news is not and never has been, because it doesn't talk about the small moments. Moments that matter to individuals, whatever they do or do not do in the grand scheme of things. And it is those individual moments that belong to people, that deserve to be faced and remembered as much as every big, world-changing disaster. And nature, because it exists in the details, is so easy to elide, even when trying to talk about it.

One day, in quarantine 2020, I sat on the back porch for hours as it rained, skipping between reading Gerard Manley Hopkins and just sitting and looking out onto the green of our small back-yard and the bushes and flowers and trees and weeds, and listen-ing to the rain. Not thinking, not hardly feeling, but just being. Perhaps a feeling did occur to me in that moment, but it was indescribable. Whatever it was, when I came inside, I knew I wanted to create an anthology of poems—eco-poetry, if you will, but with a twist; a difference in focus.

The structure of this book is that of a piece of music. The poems are placed to be read in order, with the entire piece going through movements. Certain pieces I've put back-to-back because of similarities in tone or theme, others because of subject, still others because of the effect of juxtaposition on those before and after.

In choosing what poems to put in this volume, I've tried to keep in mind a number of considerations. In essence, it all started with a feeling, that became, as I continued, a more formalized criterion. It started with "Lost Things," by Sara Teasdale. Teasdale has been one of my favorite poets ever since I first read her collections; they are so simple, straightforward, and compact, but undeniably lyrical—(she herself thought of them as songs)—tak-ing a form that could become trite and raising it to something pro-found through her ideas and ways of expressing herself. It's that *simplicity*—and simplicity of feeling—that I've tried to encapsulate throughout the volume. Which isn't to say there are no complex-ities; there are. There are tangles of every emotion, from joy and gladness, to nostalgia, fear, sadness, depression, and anguish.

The only emotion I purposefully stayed away from is anger. Not because that isn't also an important moment in human expe-rience, because it is. But on this topic, that of the environment, there has been so much already dealt with on anger, on bitterness. Sometimes, in fact, that seems all it's possible to find—both outside and in. But simple longing is so easily subsumed under more powerfully expressed emotions, and other things just as important as anger become overshadowed. Because of that stricture, I've left out some poems I considered that very much struck me (for example, Robert Burns' "The Wounded Hare" [1789]). Furthermore, I wanted to stay away from poems that were too abstract, metaphysical, theoretical; even if what they said was both interesting and pertinent; the abstract "big picture" poems tend to have a less immediate, less emotional feel, without the surprise and juxtaposition, without the experience of *running into nature*.

The other things I kept in mind as I chose poems were thematic. I wanted to, as far as possible, stay away from poems where the earth, or nature, were clearly—and only—being used as a metaphor, or where they were entirely idealized (as in much Romantic poetry). I also stayed away from poems that dealt with the undeniably *mythical* as a subject, such as mermaids. Instead I tried to stay with poems that felt immediate and real, poems where the poet is taking part in observation and action. To keep the focus on the relationship between the poet and nature, I've cut poems that are, on the one hand, descriptions of nature without a human element; and on the other hand, poems that are too focused on the human element, where nature is only a background. Instead I tried to balance between, at the precise intersection where the poet is an undeniable presence, and the subject of the poem is undeniably nature, or nature-and-the-poet; whether that's broad, like a place, or narrow, like the poet and a single animal.

I also wanted this to be a collection that, as much as possible, spanned the years since this problem began. To say that people weren't aware, from the first, of the effect the Industrial Revolution was having on nature—and on themselves—is to commit a falsehood. Both Burns (in 1791) and Gerard Manley Hopkins (in 1879) wrote, for instance, poems decrying the cutting down of trees that they had cared about; Burns going so far as to place the blame, in the poem, on exactly who was responsible, referring to the Duke of Queensberry with the lines "The worm that gnaw'd my bonie trees, / That reptile wears a ducal crown." In fact, some of Hopkins' depression in later life was specifically borne out of the soul-sucking effect of the polluted cities he worked in as Jesuit priest.

It would be remiss not to mention the religious elements in many of these poems as well, particularly the older ones. Hopkins, whose poems were the second addition to this volume and the other strand upon which I based my initial feeling of what it ought to be—visually and wordplay-rich, strikingly honest and personal, while also being more than personal—was of course explicitly religious. And in "Pied Beauty," he starts his description of the natural world with "Glory be to God for dappled things." It's something that can do with reminding, I believe—that religion and caring for the earth, even caring about conservation, are not somehow diametrical opposites. But in no way does the addition of religious poems point to an easy answer. There may be devout poets; poets with a spiritual focus but criticisms of organized religion, such as William Blake; poets who are religious yet operate outside the Western tradition, such as Rabindranath Tagore; the many more poets where their religion becomes a subtler background to their poems; and secular poets too.

Of course, as much as it might be tempting to leave everything in the past, there are also many ways in which it is only now that people are beginning to experience the full effects of what is happening to this world, and contemporary poems are an undeniable part of the picture. For these, I wanted to find poems that specifically dealt with global warming or climate change, but where that wasn't the entirety of the poem—where, as before, the heart lay in the interaction between the poet and nature.

Places that speak to people, places people have lost, ordinary places made memorable by an unexpected intersection with the natural world; people watching birds, cutting branches, raking leaves, walking along the river, sitting at home, remembering home, trying to find meaning, dealing with confusion, with grief. People adding humor to the humorless, adding the personal subjectivity of experience to the scientific fact, dealing with death, with guilt, with memory, with responsibility. People trying to imagine a way forward, and to come to terms with the idea that "there may not be a morning after" (L.L. Barkat, "When Morning Comes"). That *multitude of experience* is what this volume tries to cover, and I hope that, in some way, my selections have created a piece in which, when you read it, you might find both catharsis and challenge. Like every poet who has published something on the world, and hoped against hope it would mean something, I hope this means something. My hopes are both ambitious and small—that this might (if only!) change the world—or that this might change merely a single moment, for someone, somewhere. It would not be enough and yet, it would be enough.

Caring for the earth is not a new phenomenon, and when brought down to its simplest level, it's neither political nor religious. Religion is about specific beliefs. Politics is about the problems and solutions—or lack of them.

Caring itself, that's human.

—Sara Barkat, 2020

Lost Things

Oh, I could let the world go by,
    Its loud new wonders and its wars,
But how will I give up the sky
    When winter dusk is set with stars?

And I could let the cities go,
    Their changing customs and their creeds,—
But oh, the summer rains that blow
    In silver on the jewel-weeds!

—Sara Teasdale

God's Grandeur

The world is charged with the grandeur of God.
It will flame out, like shining from shook foil;
It gathers to a greatness, like the ooze of oil
Crushed. Why do men then now not reck his rod?
Generations have trod, have trod, have trod;
And all is seared with trade; bleared, smeared with toil;
And wears man's smudge and shares man's smell: the soil
Is bare now, nor can foot feel, being shod.

And for all this, nature is never spent;
There lives the dearest freshness deep down things;
And though the last lights off the black West went
Oh, morning, at the brown brink eastward, springs —
Because the Holy Ghost over the bent
World broods with warm breast and with ah! bright wings.

—Gerard Manley Hopkins

I wandered lonely as a cloud

I wandered lonely as a cloud
That floats on high o'er vales and hills,
When all at once I saw a crowd,
A host, of golden daffodils;
Beside the lake, beneath the trees,
Fluttering and dancing in the breeze.

Continuous as the stars that shine
And twinkle on the milky way,
They stretched in never-ending line
Along the margin of a bay:
Ten thousand saw I at a glance,
Tossing their heads in sprightly dance.

The waves beside them danced; but they
Outdid the sparkling waves in glee;
A poet could not but be gay,
In such a jocund company;
I gazed—and gazed—but little thought
What wealth the show to me had brought:

For oft, when on my couch I lie
In vacant or in pensive mood,
They flash upon that inward eye
Which is the bliss of solitude;
And then my heart with pleasure fills,
And dances with the daffodils.

—William Wordsworth

Inversnaid

This darksome burn, horseback brown,
His rollrock highroad roaring down,
In coop and in comb the fleece of his foam
Flutes and low to the lake falls home.

A windpuff-bonnet of fáwn-fróth
Turns and twindles over the broth
Of a pool so pitchblack, féll-frówning,
It rounds and rounds Despair to drowning.

Degged with dew, dappled with dew
Are the groins of the braes that the brook treads through,
Wiry heathpacks, flitches of fern,
And the beadbonny ash that sits over the burn.

What would the world be, once bereft
Of wet and of wildness? Let them be left,
O let them be left, wildness and wet;
Long live the weeds and the wilderness yet.

—Gerard Manley Hopkins

Places

Places I love come back to me like music,
    Hush me and heal me when I am very tired;
I see the oak woods at Saxton's flaming
    In a flare of crimson by the frost newly fired;
And I am thirsty for the spring in the valley
    As for a kiss ungiven and long desired.

I know a bright world of snowy hills at Boonton,
    A blue and white dazzling light on everything one sees,
The ice-covered branches of the hemlocks sparkle
    Bending low and tinkling in the sharp thin breeze,
And iridescent crystals fall and crackle on the snow-crust
    With the winter sun drawing cold blue shadows from
        the trees.

Violet now, in veil on veil of evening
    The hills across from Cromwell grow dreamy and far;
A wood-thrush is singing soft as a viol
    In the heart of the hollow where the dark pools are;
The primrose has opened her pale yellow flowers
    And heaven is lighting star after star.

Places I love come back to me like music—
    Mid-ocean, midnight, the waves buzz drowsily;
In the ship's deep churning the eerie phosphorescence
    Is like the souls of people who were drowned at sea,
And I can hear a man's voice, speaking, hushed, insistent,
    At midnight, in mid-ocean, hour on hour to me.

—Sara Teasdale

The Lake Isle of Innisfree

I will arise and go now, and go to Innisfree,
And a small cabin build there, of clay and wattles made:
Nine bean-rows will I have there, a hive for the honey-bee,
And live alone in the bee-loud glade.

And I shall have some peace there, for peace comes dropping slow,
Dropping from the veils of the morning to where the cricket sings;
There midnight's all a glimmer, and noon a purple glow,
And evening full of the linnet's wings.

I will arise and go now, for always night and day
I hear lake water lapping with low sounds by the shore;
While I stand on the roadway, or on the pavements grey,
I hear it in the deep heart's core.

—William Butler Yeats

The Cypress Broke

*The cypress is the tree's grief and not
the tree, and it has no shadow because it is
the tree's shadow*
     Bassam Hajjar

The cypress broke like a minaret, and slept on
the road upon its chapped shadow, dark, green,
as it has always been. No one got hurt. The vehicles
sped over its branches. The dust blew
into the windshields… / The cypress broke, but
the pigeon in a neighboring house didn't change
its public nest. And two migrant birds hovered above
the hem of the place, and exchanged some symbols.
And a woman said to her neighbor: Say, did you see a storm?
She said: No, and no bulldozer either… / And the cypress
broke. And those passing by the wreckage said:
Maybe it got bored with being neglected, or it grew old
with the days, it is long like a giraffe, and little
in meaning like a dust broom, and couldn't shade two lovers.
And a boy said: I used to draw it perfectly,
its figure was easy to draw. And a girl said: The sky today
is incomplete because the cypress broke.
And a young man said: But the sky today is complete
because the cypress broke. And I said
to myself: Neither mystery nor clarity,
the cypress broke, and that is all
there is to it: the cypress broke!

—Mahmoud Darwish

"It's been three years"

It's been three years
Since my neighbor chopped down
The fig tree on the other side of the fence
It's been three years since my peach tree hasn't flowered
On this side of the fence …

—Irakli Kakabadze

Verses On The Destruction Of The Woods Near Drumlanrig

As on the banks o' wandering Nith,
    Ae smiling simmer morn I stray'd,
And traced its bonie howes and haughs,
    Where linties sang and lammies play'd,
I sat me down upon a craig,
    And drank my fill o' fancy's dream,
When from the eddying deep below,
    Up rose the genius of the stream.

Dark, like the frowning rock, his brow,
    And troubled, like his wintry wave,
And deep, as sughs the boding wind
    Amang his caves, the sigh he gave—
"And come ye here, my son," he cried,
    "To wander in my birken shade?
To muse some favourite Scottish theme,
    Or sing some favourite Scottish maid?

"There was a time, it's nae lang syne,
    Ye might hae seen me in my pride,
When a' my banks sae bravely saw
    Their woody pictures in my tide;
When hanging beech and spreading elm
    Shaded my stream sae clear and cool:
And stately oaks their twisted arms
    Threw broad and dark across the pool;

"When, glinting thro' the trees, appear'd
   The wee white cot aboon the mill,
And peacefu' rose its ingle reek,
   That, slowly curling, clamb the hill.
But now the cot is bare and cauld,
   Its leafy bield for ever gane,
And scarce a stinted birk is left
   To shiver in the blast its lane."

"Alas!" quoth I, "what ruefu' chance
   Has twin'd ye o' your stately trees?
Has laid your rocky bosom bare—
   Has stripped the cleeding o' your braes?
Was it the bitter eastern blast,
   That scatters blight in early spring?
Or was't the wil'fire scorch'd their boughs,
   Or canker-worm wi' secret sting?"

"Nae eastlin blast," the sprite replied;
   "It blaws na here sae fierce and fell,
And on my dry and halesome banks
   Nae canker-worms get leave to dwell:
Man! cruel man!" the genius sighed—
   As through the cliffs he sank him down—
"The worm that gnaw'd my bonie trees,
   That reptile wears a ducal crown."

—Robert Burns

Binsey Poplars

felled 1879

My aspens dear, whose airy cages quelled,
Quelled or quenched in leaves the leaping sun,
All felled, felled, are all felled;
Of a fresh and following folded rank
Not spared, not one
That dandled a sandalled
Shadow that swam or sank
On meadow and river and wind-wandering weed-winding bank.

O if we but knew what we do
When we delve or hew —
Hack and rack the growing green!
Since country is so tender
To touch, her being só slender,
That, like this sleek and seeing ball
But a prick will make no eye at all,
Where we, even where we mean
To mend her we end her,
When we hew or delve:
After-comers cannot guess the beauty been.
Ten or twelve, only ten or twelve
Strokes of havoc únselve
The sweet especial scene,
Rural scene, a rural scene,
Sweet especial rural scene.

—Gerard Manley Hopkins

The Garden of Love

I went to the Garden of Love,
And saw what I never had seen:
A Chapel was built in the midst,
Where I used to play on the green.

And the gates of this Chapel were shut,
And Thou shalt not. writ over the door;
So I turn'd to the Garden of Love,
That so many sweet flowers bore.

And I saw it was filled with graves,
And tomb-stones where flowers should be:
And Priests in black gowns, were walking their rounds,
And binding with briars, my joys & desires.

—William Blake

Late Summer

Before the moths have even appeared
to orbit around them, the streetlamps come on,
a long row of them glowing uselessly

along the ring of garden that circles the city center,
where your steps count down the dulling of daylight.
At your feet, a bee crawls in small circles like a toy unwinding.

Summer specializes in time, slows it down almost to dream.
And the noisy day goes so quiet you can hear
the bedraggled man who visits each trash receptacle

mutter in disbelief: *Everything in the world is being thrown away!*
Summer lingers, but it's about ending. It's about how things
redden and ripen and burst and come down. It's when

city workers cut down trees, demolishing
one limb at a time, spilling the crumbs
of twigs and leaves all over the tablecloth of street.

Sunglasses! the man softly exclaims
while beside him blooms a large gray rose of pigeons
huddled around a dropped piece of bread.

—Jennifer Grotz

Pied Beauty

Glory be to God for dappled things—
    For skies of couple-colour as a brinded cow;
    For rose-moles all in stipple upon trout that swim;
Fresh-firecoal chestnut-falls; finches' wings;
    Landscape plotted and pieced—fold, fallow, and plough;
    And áll trádes, their gear and tackle and trim.
All things counter, original, spare, strange;
    Whatever is fickle, freckled (who knows how?)
    With swift, slow; sweet, sour; adazzle, dim;
He fathers-forth whose beauty is past change:
                Praise him.

—Gerard Manley Hopkins

Before Dark

From the porch at dusk I watched
a kingfisher wild in flight
he could only have made for joy.

He came down the river, splashing
against the water's dimming face
like a skipped rock, passing

on down out of sight. And still
I could hear the splashes
farther and farther away

as it grew darker. He came back
the same way, dusky as his shadow,
sudden beyond the willows.

The splashes went on out of hearing.
It was dark then. Somewhere
the night had accommodated him

—at the place he was headed for
or where, led by his delight,
he came.

—Wendell Berry

Birds in Home Depot—December

They sing, staccato notes:
statements that could be,
queer tree, queer tree…

Sometimes I see them
brown dots on a brown beam.

No easy nest here,
the spruce branches broken,
straw sequestered tight in brooms
wrapped in cellophane,

except for the threadbare Fall
scarecrow, braced firmly
among the colored corn stalks
and baskets of stippled gourds.

I want them to see the irony
under the steel beams
where they hop and fly, searching—
the fragments of a home
imagined new, repaired, changed.

In the garden center, a sparrow
contemplates the crocus bulbs,
huddled on shelves, awaiting Spring,
under the canopy that lets
in the sky and cool air.

I've wandered these aisles,
like today with my scribbled list,
unable to find a pin for a screen
door, a number four brass screw
for a fan, a summer breeze.

What does that weaver know,
I wonder, as he tugs at browned
lily leaves and with a torn fragment flies
out the wide opened doors.

—Richard Maxson

Dust of Snow

The way a crow
Shook down on me
The dust of snow
From a hemlock tree

Has given my heart
A change of mood
And saved some part
Of a day I had rued.

—Robert Frost

Midnight Sun

at approximately 59° 45' N Latitude, 154° 55' W Longitude

Each night,
I watch the sun set
over Lake Iliamna
through the willows.
How physical:
the names of willows:
Bebb and Scouler,
feltleaf, arctic, undergreen—
names ill-suited for their frail appearance.
And how palpable the story,
told by the black-capped chickadee
about the four bears who come
each night to the village,
linger for a couple of hours,
then vanish.
As the bird now vanishes
from atop the satellite dish
outside the room at Gram's B&B.
He leaves behind
a white remembrance,
which disturbs the signal
coming from Anchorage,
interrupting a program about
the formation of the Hawai'ian Islands,
and sending ripples of multi-colored "snow"
swirling into TV screen volcanoes.
While back outside,
midsummer sun barely sets on the village,

angling over sparse willows
and spruce, bentgrass and sweetgale,
perhaps twinflower, although
verifying the presence of that species
may require a second look.
A second look, which the sun
will suggest, upon its return
four and one-half hours from now.
That is when the BLM surveyors will arrive
on their ATVs (whatever the weather
and whether they're foolish or clever),
to verify yesterday's measurements,
as they do each morning,
in this village of willows
and midnight sun.

—Scott Edward Anderson

The Owl

The owl is here.
He perches on the wall. And meditates.
Whose death does he announce
if no one lives in this village?
The fossils of the people
do not cross to either side.

The tombs in the cemetery paint the moon
that has begun to chew the underbrush.
The owl
rehearses a song to life.
It refuses to presage its own death.

—Briceida Cuevas Cob

Lost Lake

A soggy brightness at the northernmost ridge
of the Tahkenitch, even nearing dusk and not
a Domino's for miles. I said holy at a coniferous wall
of western hemlock overhead and red cedar
which rose up from the foot of that costal creek
bearing its image and all around. I had not known
I'd come as a witness. The great Pacific rolled in
news from distant shores beyond a stretch of dune
trails behind us. White-winged gulls shrieked
and flapped at our misery frothing in waves.

—Major Jackson

The Wood-Pile

Out walking in the frozen swamp one gray day,
I paused and said, 'I will turn back from here.
No, I will go on farther—and we shall see.'
The hard snow held me, save where now and then
One foot went through. The view was all in lines
Straight up and down of tall slim trees
Too much alike to mark or name a place by
So as to say for certain I was here
Or somewhere else: I was just far from home.
A small bird flew before me. He was careful
To put a tree between us when he lighted,
And say no word to tell me who he was
Who was so foolish as to think what *he* thought.
He thought that I was after him for a feather—
The white one in his tail; like one who takes
Everything said as personal to himself.
One flight out sideways would have undeceived him.
And then there was a pile of wood for which
I forgot him and let his little fear
Carry him off the way I might have gone,
Without so much as wishing him good-night.
He went behind it to make his last stand.
It was a cord of maple, cut and split
And piled—and measured, four by four by eight.
And not another like it could I see.
No runner tracks in this year's snow looped near it.
And it was older sure than this year's cutting,
Or even last year's or the year's before.
The wood was gray and the bark warping off it
And the pile somewhat sunken. Clematis

Had wound strings round and round it like a bundle.
What held it though on one side was a tree
Still growing, and on one a stake and prop,
These latter about to fall. I thought that only
Someone who lived in turning to fresh tasks
Could so forget his handiwork on which
He spent himself, the labor of his ax,
And leave it there far from a useful fireplace
To warm the frozen swamp as best it could
With the slow smokeless burning of decay.

—Robert Frost

Tornado Warning/JoAnn Fabric & Craft

—There is desire & there is experience
says the sales manager, his speech mock
thespian beneath the siren-laced gales—

Swayed by last weekend's empowerment seminar,
he's just called Corporate to quit. Thus after Valentine
rush, farewell to the service alcove where we shelter;
farewell quilters, O exiles of the pattern workshop.
Watery Gregorian chants sound in the walls & wind

regurgitates up fountain pipes, yet the quilters
refuse to be comrades in fear; humorless, calmly
thumbing calico squares stacked on their laps.

A bully mother has sent me, again, to fetch supplies
for her holiday class party. In my basket—25 pairs
of Googly Eyes. All parents will receive awkward
crimson hearts that blink in surprise at our boredom.
The manager rests his head on bolts of jade toile,

already gone to study costume design, four cities away.
Unseasonal storms dare not upset this fabric's pastoral:
shepherds court maidens, lutes forgotten in the meadows.

—Martha Greenwald

Jet

Sometimes I wish I were still out
on the back porch, drinking jet fuel
with the boys, getting louder and louder
as the empty cans drop out of our paws
like booster rockets falling back to Earth

and we soar up into the summer stars.
Summer. The big sky river rushes overhead,
bearing asteroids and mist, blind fish
and old space suits with skeletons inside.
On Earth, men celebrate their hairiness,

and it is good, a way of letting life
out of the box, uncapping the bottle
to let the effervescence gush
through the narrow, usually constricted neck.

And now the crickets plug in their appliances
in unison, and then the fireflies flash
dots and dashes in the grass, like punctuation
for the labyrinthine, untrue tales of sex
someone is telling in the dark, though

no one really hears. We gaze into the night
as if remembering the bright unbroken planet
we once came from,
to which we will never
be permitted to return.
We are amazed how hurt we are.
We would give anything for what we have.

—Tony Hoagland

"On the day when the lotus bloomed, alas, my mind was straying"

On the day when the lotus bloomed, alas, my mind was straying, and I knew it not. My basket was empty and the flower remained unheeded.

Only now and again a sadness fell upon me, and I started up from my dream and felt a sweet trace of a strange fragrance in the south wind.

That vague sweetness made my heart ache with longing and it seemed to me that it was the eager breath of the summer seeking for its completion.

I knew not then that it was so near, that it was mine, and that this perfect sweetness had blossomed in the depth of my own heart.

—Rabindranath Tagore

Beefsteak

You must grow your own miracles.
Special has been hormoned
and hardened against the bump
and bruise. Pretty in the produce
aisle, but pithless and pitiful.

I prefer a nude stocking sling
for the heft, a slow blush,
not the red-on-arrival rouge
needled in the green-to-go.

In a hot June—the prize, only
once a year, the furrowed fruit
weighs down its stems for clipping
in your open hand, quite full
of tender skin. Take care carrying
them to the kitchen, prepare
the bed of lettuce or only bread
and mayo, and oh! say a prayer before
you slice a single slice and lay
the flawless redness down and bite.

—Richard Maxson

Jonah's Revenge

Oh, to swim with the great blues,
diving and diving, in grace,
where the chilled krill live
and inching up to breathless air,

where blue baleens, toothless,
chomp on a prophet, abandoned
action figures, and seasoned
Styrofoam that will endure

long beyond salted whalebone
scrimshaw, yet, sorrow fails
to deter the roundelays of rorquals
awash in nylon webs, their wails

unheard back on land where
a wind-up whale, a tub toy diving
in bath bubbles, affirms our hapless
notion that all life is but whimsy.

—Sandra Fox Murphy

In my defense, there was a very dense fog

I thought the moon was hanging over
my left shoulder, a welcome light
on a dark drive before sunup.

Turns out it was the headlight
of a car behind me, double
bounced, first from my rearview
then to the droplets sprayed
across the side window's glass.

—Will Willingham

Fashion Victim

Too much mist to see the mountain. The freeway
lost in fog. The garden—a mirage. I order clothes
all day from catalogues—(a bird

flies into a cloud
and never flies back out)—like

a passenger on a doomed flight, raising
her glass in a toast
to the pilot, to the sky. They arrive

in long white boxes and in whispers
on the porch, like winter. Soon

there will be nothing but obscurity
as far as the eye can see. Until

there's only one leaf left

clinging to one tree. Until, like

my father over there in his chair, my
clothes are how you know it's me.

—Laura Kasischke

A Chair on a Highway on a Rainy Afternoon

a velvet chair
        standing by itself
            on a highway
a chair standing by itself on a highway
        means its life is over
a life of ups and downs
        before it was brought here
            and left beside the grass
nevertheless
        it was laid down squarely
                maybe
                        thanks to a final gesture of love
with all four legs standing against the asphalt
this whisks an image to my mind:
        a wandering soul who leisurely sits here
                between the passing cars
                and the mud
but surely no soul can be so foolish
    as to come and sit on a torn old abandoned chair
        on a dark cold rainy September afternoon
            on a lightless highway
or
to give the chair
a little consolation
I conclude as follows:

        there exists such a soul
        it's just that he, or she, is
            not here
            not now

—P. K.

Poetry Slam

Come to think of it, there was
something strangely poetic
about the raccoon standing
in front of the Chevy

on two iambic feet, enjambed
across the glowing center line—
his eyes frozen blank
like a verse in headlights
pooled on the pavement
eager to receive his fresh offering.

A defiant thought flashed
across black-masked eyes
at the sound of the tires' screech,

I'm not about to be a
jail-striped elegy.

—Will Willingham

Marshlands

A thin wet sky, that yellows at the rim,
And meets with sun-lost lip the marsh's brim.

The pools low lying, dank with moss and mould,
Glint through their mildews like large cups of gold.

Among the wild rice in the still lagoon,
In monotone the lizard shrills his tune.

The wild goose, homing, seeks a sheltering,
Where rushes grow, and oozing lichens cling.

Late cranes with heavy wing, and lazy flight,
Sail up the silence with the nearing night.

And like a spirit, swathed in some soft veil,
Steals twilight and its shadows o'er the swale.

Hushed lie the sedges, and the vapours creep,
Thick, grey and humid, while the marshes sleep.

—Emily Pauline Johnson

Matsiranna

On the veranda of this house dries a lone hogweed. In the yard scuttle more ticks than the average body would accommodate. Around this house is a forest that is at once dense and spacious, a forest like in a good horror film. Opening beyond the forest is the frameless door of the sea. Ever since the former Pioneer camp was used for prison guards' summer outings, plastic cups started sprouting on the beach. They did not affect the feeling that voluntary solitude is still possible for a while longer.

—Jan Kaus

Dead River Road

Morning light strobes through the tree line, picks up frost-glitter over the sturdy frame—a deer carcass picked clean. Rooted to the backbones, ribs arc over a hollow, protect a heart that disintegrated some time ago.

I slow my car to get a closer look, but there's no shoulder along the road. No stopping. No standing. The woods on either side are posted, *No Trespassing.*

—Michelle Ortega

Leaving Tulsa

for Cosetta

Once there were coyotes, cardinals
in the cedar. You could cure amnesia
with the trees of our back-forty. Once
I drowned in a monsoon of frogs—
Grandma said it was a good thing, a promise
for a good crop. Grandma's perfect tomatoes.
Squash. She taught us to shuck corn, laughing,
never spoke about her childhood
or the faces in gingerbread tins
stacked in the closet.

She was covered in a quilt, the Creek way.
But I don't know this kind of burial:
vanishing toads, thinning pecan groves,
peach trees choked by palms.
New neighbors tossing clipped grass
over our fence line, griping to the city
of our overgrown fields.

Grandma fell in love with a truck driver,
grew watermelons by the pond
on our Indian allotment,
took us fishing for dragonflies.
When the bulldozers came
with their documents from the city
and a truckload of pipelines,
her shotgun was already loaded.

Under the bent chestnut, the well
where Cosetta's husband
hid his whiskey—buried beneath roots
her bundle of beads. *They tell*
the story of our family. Cosetta's land
flattened to a parking lot.

Grandma potted a cedar sapling
I could take on the road for luck.
She used the bark for heart lesions
doctors couldn't explain.
To her they were maps, traces of home,
the Milky Way, where she's going, she said.

After the funeral
I stowed her jewelry in the ground,
promised to return when the rivers rose.

On the grassy plain behind the house
one buffalo remains.

Along the highway's gravel pits
sunflowers stand in dense rows.
Telephone poles crook into the layered sky.
A crow's beak broken by a windmill's blade.
It is then I understand my grandmother:
When they see open land
they only know to take it.

I understand how to walk among hay bales
looking for turtle shells.
How to sing over the groan of the county road
widening to four lanes.
I understand how to keep from looking up:
small planes trail overhead
as I kneel in the Johnson grass
combing away footprints.

Up here, parallel to the median
with a vista of mesas' weavings,
the sky a belt of blue and white beadwork,
I see our hundred and sixty acres
stamped on God's forsaken country,
a roof blown off a shed,
beams bent like matchsticks,
a drove of white cows
making their home
in a derailed train car.

—Jennifer Elise Foerster

Dam

I guess I hoped for
   a single outcome,
      water rushing
         only my way
      and somehow
         not leaving
            the others
         high and dry

—Will Willingham

On Meeting an Old German Woman by the Hudson River

"Even on a day like this,"
she said,
"I have to come out here."

   (*some fish and crabs*
   from these waters may be
   dangerous to eat, they posted
   near the rocks where today
   no one is fishing)

Even on a day like this, bitter, gray,
she responds to me:
"Yes, it's beautiful."

I tell her about the birds I saw,
white with black-capped heads—
their heads so round, so very very round.

    (I do not tell her I culled from the sand,
    where the driftwood has washed in:
    two plastic caps, two straws,
    two broken pens—one saying
    Chase Bank—a shrunken plastic
    water bottle, shard of yellow plate,
    square of Styrofoam)

"I love it when they fly," she told me.

Her eyes were blue as the sky is not today.
Her hat was forest, by the treeless water's edge.
Her coat was cranberry,
and as she walked away I forgot to think
how much she looked like a holiday
moving down the shore.

—L.L. Barkat

Carrizo

For Edgar

The submarine's inside was dim.
— Ryūnosuke Akutagawa, tr. by Will Petersen

in my youth, I hitched a ride to San Diego, across
chirping desert and distant night, I gazed upon a slow-moving
dark, encasing a convex cerulean cavity

each night, I stood beneath the sky for hours mesmerized
at the perplex reformatory, twinkling lights of broken
glass fragments spreading against a glistening sunset

a faceless man behind a lost reflection of glass
at a drive-up window informs me,
too bad, you know nothing of your own past

how far will I walk against the night?
conforming to a captivity I had never realized

some years later, under the kitchen table, they all huddle,
as the rampage continues toward the back of the house,
a clash of debris from the other room recoils
and broken sounds escape the barricade of doors

I remember I returned in 1970,
all they remember is me sitting at the edge of my bed,
with the war still in my hands

—Crisosto Apache

Shadows on the Snow

The snow comes late this year. Violet shadows
doze like shepherds round
a white fire.
The swaying shadow of a fence looks like a woman's clavicle—
a woman who dreams of her lover's snowy journey home,
his late return.

Thin trails lead to the doorway.
A car parked for hours
compresses black earth.
Radio signals float just out of earshot.
A boat with its eel fishers
in luminous raincoats skims by.
A child—his little hand trembling—
casts slanting trees across the table.

The choir kneels.
The moment has come to speak
in a voice I have never known before.

I raise my head and see a single star in the night sky,
shapeless and fearful like the shard of a broken bottleneck,
a star I have for years foolishly followed.
Perhaps the shadow of our infinite persistence
looks to someone else like a large hump
on the Moon
a camel bent over a puddle
preparing for a new stretch of thirst.

—Luljeta Lleshanaku

Degrees of Blue

At the place in the story

where a knock on the hull wakes the dreamer
and he opens his eyes to find the rowers gone,
the boat tied to an empty dock,

the boy looks up from his book,

out the window, and sees
the hills have turned their backs,
they are walking into evening.

How long does he watch them go?
Does the part of him that follows
call for years across his growing sadness?

When he returns to the tale,
the page is dark,

and the leaves at the window have been traveling
beside his silent reading
as long as he can remember.

Where is his father?
When will his mother be home?

How is he going to explain
the moon taken hostage, the sea
risen to fill up all the mirrors?

How is he going to explain the branches
beginning to grow from his ribs and throat,
the cries and trills starting in his own mouth?

And now that ancient sorrow between his hips,
his body's ripe listening
the planet
knowing itself at last.

—Li-Young Lee

My Awe Is a Weakness

I stood before the TV like a wall of stone.
My network of nerves blacked out.
I should have been chiseling a garden.
I should have chartered a new thought
for a far-off reader imprisoned in his future suburbia.
The evening sky flashed its high definition.
All was night-goggle green, even later her eyes,
which made us aliens unto each other,
and when we went to touch one another as before
like stained glass, nothing flared in us, nothing.

—Major Jackson

I Shall Return

I shall return again; I shall return
To laugh and love and watch with wonder-eyes
At golden noon the forest fires burn,
Wafting their blue-black smoke to sapphire skies.
I shall return to loiter by the streams
That bathe the brown blades of the bending grasses,
And realize once more my thousand dreams
Of waters rushing down the mountain passes.
I shall return to hear the fiddle and fife
Of village dances, dear delicious tunes
That stir the hidden depths of native life,
Stray melodies of dim remembered runes.
I shall return, I shall return again,
To ease my mind of long, long years of pain.

—Claude McKay

Living with the News

Can I get used to it day after day
a little at a time while the tide keeps
coming in faster the waves get bigger
building on each other breaking records
this is not the world that I remember
then comes the day when I open the box
that I remember packing with such care
and there is the face that I had known well
in little pieces staring up at me
it is not mentioned on the front pages
but somewhere far back near the real estate
among the things that happen every day
to someone who now happens to be me
and what can I do and who can tell me
then there is what the doctor comes to say
endless patience will never be enough
the only hope is to be the daylight

—W. S. Merwin

Return to Sloansville

I close my eyes,
blot out one hundred
and fifty shale driveways
pickup trucks, Ford
Pintos, trailers barely
tied to this ground
by wires, gas lines
cable TV.

I can still see
dirt road, Queen
Anne's Lace, goldenrod
blue chicory,
field mice nesting
under leaning timothy
and the apple orchard
rooted beyond tall firs

where a woman
in navy sweat pants
and red Budweiser t-shirt
is just now hanging laundry
to drift upon the wind,
sing with ghosts
of spring white
blossoms, honeybees.

—L. L. Barkat

If You Return Alone

If you return alone, tell yourself:
Exile has changed its features…
Wasn't Abu Tammam before you harrowed
when he met himself:
"Neither you are you
nor home is home"…

Things will carry for you your patriotic feeling:
A wildflower will sprout in your abandoned corner /
The house sparrow will pick at the letter "h"
in your name
in the fig tree's broken husk /
A bee will sting your hand as you reach
for the goose fuzz behind this fence /

As for you,
the mirror has failed you,
and you are… and aren't you:
Where did I leave my face? you say
then search for your feeling, outside the things,
between a crying happiness and a guffawing depression…
Have you found yourself now?
Tell yourself: I returned alone missing
two moons,
but home is home!

—Mahmoud Darwish

Dreaming Backwards

Pale pink peaches, cut syrup-sweet
sticking on fingers; jarred in clean cans sparkle-bright,
crisp, snapping cracking apples tumbling into cider-press
Remembering. The tragedy of un-thinned lettuce
too enamoured of small soft sprigs—
garden beds full of weeds; lawn of clover and violet.
Still a sustenance of green—every year through
drought, frost, rain, unseasonable snow.
Life despite. The honey-wings of bees, bending branches
stolen by squirrels, hummingbird sipping sugar
pumpkin-petaled monarch—a place to rest.
Just for a while.

—Sara Barkat

Scent
of death upon
the leaves;
how lovely
the fragrance.

—L.L. Barkat

I Pity the Garden

No one thinks of the flowers.
No one thinks of the fish.
No one wants to believe the garden is dying,
that its heart has swollen in the heat
of this sun, that its mind drains slowly
of its lush memories.

Our garden is forlorn.
It yawns waiting
for rain from a stray cloud
and our pond sits empty,
callow stars bite the dust
from atop tall trees
and from the pale home of the fish
comes the hack of coughing every night.

Our garden is forlorn.

Father says: *My time is past*
my time is past,
I've carried my burden
I'm done with my work.
He stays in his room from dawn to dusk
reads History of Histories or Ferdowsi's Epic of Kings.

Father says to Mother:
Damn every fish and every bird!
When I'm dead, what will it matter
if the garden lives or dies.
My pension
is all that counts.

Mother's life is a rolled out prayer rug.
She lives in terror of hell, always seeks
Sin's footprints in every corner,
imagines the garden sullied
by the sin of a wayward plant.

Mother is a sinner by nature. She prays
all day, then with her "consecrated" breath
blows on all the flowers, all the fish
and all over her own body.
She awaits the Promised One and
the forgiveness He is to bring.

My brother calls the garden a graveyard.
He laughs at the plight of the grass
and ruthlessly counts the corpses of the fish
rotting beneath the sick skin of shallow water.
My brother is addicted to philosophy
he sees the healing of the garden in its death.
Drunk, he beats his fists on doors and walls
says he is tired, pained and despondent.
He carries his despair everywhere,
just as he carries his birth certificate
diary, napkin, lighter and pen.

But his despair is so small
that each night it is lost
in crowded taverns.

My sister was a friend to flowers.
She would take her simple heart's words
—when Mother beat her—
to their kind and silent gathering

and sometimes she would treat the family
of fish to sunshine and cake crumbs.

She now lives on the other side of town
in her artificial home
and in the arms of her artificial husband
she makes natural children.
Each time she visits us, if her skirt is sullied
with the poverty of our garden
she bathes herself in perfume.
Every time she visits she is with child.

Our garden is forlorn
Our garden is forlorn

All day from behind the door
come sounds of cuts and tears
sounds of blasts.
Our neighbors plant bombs and machine guns,
instead of flowers, in their garden soil.
They cover their ponds, hiding bags of gunpowder.

The school children fill their backpacks
with tiny bombs.

Our garden is dizzy.

I fear the age that has lost its heart,
the idleness of so many hands
the alienation in so many faces.

I am like a schoolchild madly
in love with her geometry books.
I am forlorn

and imagine it is possible to take the garden to a hospital.
I imagine I imagine
And the garden's heart has swollen in the heat
of this sun, its mind slowly drains of its lush memories.

—Forugh Farrokhzad

The Egoist

No one missing from the garden. No one here:
only winter, green and black, the day
sleepless as an apparition,
a white phantom, in shivers,
on the castle steps. The hour
when no one arrives, when drops
coagulating in the sprinkle
on naked winter trees now and then fall
and I and you in this solitary zone,
invincible and alone, keep hoping
no one arrives, no, that no one comes
bearing a smile or medal or pretext
to propose something to us.

It's the hour
when leaves fall, triturated
across the ground, when
out of being and unbeing they return to their source,
their gold and green stripped away
until they've gone to root again

and again, undone and reborn,
they lift their heads into spring.
Oh heart lost
within me, in my own investiture,
what sweet modulations people you!
I'm neither culpable
for running away nor for being saved:
misery couldn't wear me down!
Though gusto can sour
if it's kissed every day,
and no one shakes free
from the sun but by dying.

What can I do if the star picked me
for its lightning, and if the thorn
pointed out to me the pain of all those others.
What can I do if every gesture
of my hand drew me closer to the rose?
Must I apologize for this winter,
the most remote, the most unapproachable
for that man who turned his face to the cold
though no one suffered for his happiness?

And if along these roads
—far-off France, foggy numbers—
I return to the precincts of my life:
a solitary garden, a poor quarter,
and suddenly this day like every other
runs down stairs that don't exist
dressed in irresistible purity,
and there's an odor of biting solitude,
of humidity, of water, of rebirth:

what can I do if I breathe by myself,
why will I feel cut to the quick?

—Pablo Neruda

Christmas Trees

(A Christmas Circular Letter)

The city had withdrawn into itself
And left at last the country to the country;
When between whirls of snow not come to lie
And whirls of foliage not yet laid, there drove
A stranger to our yard, who looked the city,
Yet did in country fashion in that there
He sat and waited till he drew us out
A-buttoning coats to ask him who he was.
He proved to be the city come again
To look for something it had left behind
And could not do without and keep its Christmas.
He asked if I would sell my Christmas trees;
My woods—the young fir balsams like a place
Where houses all are churches and have spires.
I hadn't thought of them as Christmas Trees.
I doubt if I was tempted for a moment
To sell them off their feet to go in cars
And leave the slope behind the house all bare,
Where the sun shines now no warmer than the moon.
I'd hate to have them know it if I was.
Yet more I'd hate to hold my trees except
As others hold theirs or refuse for them,

Beyond the time of profitable growth,
The trial by market everything must come to.
I dallied so much with the thought of selling.
Then whether from mistaken courtesy
And fear of seeming short of speech, or whether
From hope of hearing good of what was mine, I said,
"There aren't enough to be worth while."
"I could soon tell how many they would cut,
You let me look them over."

         "You could look.
But don't expect I'm going to let you have them."
Pasture they spring in, some in clumps too close
That lop each other of boughs, but not a few
Quite solitary and having equal boughs
All round and round. The latter he nodded "Yes" to,
Or paused to say beneath some lovelier one,
With a buyer's moderation, "That would do."
I thought so too, but wasn't there to say so.
We climbed the pasture on the south, crossed over,
And came down on the north.
        He said, "A thousand."

"A thousand Christmas trees!—at what apiece?"

He felt some need of softening that to me:
"A thousand trees would come to thirty dollars."

Then I was certain I had never meant
To let him have them. Never show surprise!
But thirty dollars seemed so small beside
The extent of pasture I should strip, three cents
(For that was all they figured out apiece),

Three cents so small beside the dollar friends
I should be writing to within the hour
Would pay in cities for good trees like those,
Regular vestry-trees whole Sunday Schools
Could hang enough on to pick off enough.
A thousand Christmas trees I didn't know I had!
Worth three cents more to give away than sell,
As may be shown by a simple calculation.
Too bad I couldn't lay one in a letter.
I can't help wishing I could send you one,
In wishing you herewith a Merry Christmas.

—Robert Frost

Tree

It is foolish
to let a young redwood
grow next to a house.

Even in this
one lifetime,
you will have to choose.

That great calm being,
this clutter of soup pots and books—

Already the first branch-tips brush at the window.
Softly, calmly, immensity taps at your life.

—Jane Hirshfield

The Sabbath Of The Woods

Sundown—and silence—and deep peace,—
Night's benediction and release;—
The tints of day die out and cease.

This morn I heard the Sabbath bells
Across the breezy upland swells;—
My path lay down the woodland dells.

To-day, I said, the dust of creeds,
The wind of words reach not my needs;—
I worship with the birds and weeds.

From height to height the sunbeam sprung,
The wild vine, touched with vermeil, clung,
The mountain brooklet leapt and sung.

The white lamp of the lily made
A tender light in deepest shade,—
The solitary place was glad.

The very air was tremulous,—
I felt its deep and reverent hush,—
God burned before me in the bush!

And nature prayed with folded palm,
And looks that wear perpetual calm,—
The while glad notes uplifted psalm.

The wild rose swung her fragrant vase,
The daisy answered from her place,—
Praise Him whose looks are full of grace.

And violets murmured where the feet
Of brooks made hollows cool and deep;
He giveth His beloved sleep.

Wide stood the great cathedral doors,
Arched o'er with heaven's radiant floors;—
Nature, with lifted brow, adores.

And wave, and wind, and rocking trees,
And voice of birds, and hum of bees,
Made anthem, like the roll of seas.

The sunset vapors sail and swim;—
All day uprose their mighty hymn,—
I listened till the woods were dim.

And through the beechen aisles there fell
A silver silence, like a spell.
The heifer's home returning bell,

Faint and remote, as if it grew
A portion of that silence too,
Dissolved and ceased, like falling dew.

Stars twinkled through the coming night,—
A voice dropped down the purple height,—
At even time it shall be light.

Ah rest my soul, for God is good,
Though sometimes faintly understood,
His goodness fills the solitude.

Fold up thy spirit,—trust the right,

As blossoms fold their leaves at night,
And trust the sun though out of sight.

—Kate Seymour Maclean

Reply to People

Happened upon a pine forest   Rock
beneath   perfect pillow for sleep
No calendar sun   within mountains
cold ends   year   unknown

—Hermit Tai Shang

The Peace of Wild Things

When despair for the world grows in me
and I wake in the night at the least sound
in fear of what my life and my children's lives may be,
I go and lie down where the wood drake
rests in his beauty on the water, and the great heron feeds.
I come into the peace of wild things
who do not tax their lives with forethought
of grief. I come into the presence of still water.
And I feel above me the day-blind stars
waiting with their light. For a time
I rest in the grace of the world, and am free.

—Wendell Berry

The New Moon

Day, you have bruised and beaten me,
As rain beats down the bright, proud sea,
Beaten my body, bruised my soul,
Left me nothing lovely or whole—
Yet I have wrested a gift from you,
Day that dies in dusky blue:

For suddenly over the factories
I saw a moon in the cloudy seas—
A wisp of beauty all alone
In a world as hard and gray as stone—
Oh who could be bitter and want to die
When a maiden moon wakes up in the sky?

—Sara Teasdale

The Edge

I.

I thought to die that night in the solitude
    where they would never find me...
But there was time...
And I lay quietly on the drawn knees of the mountain
    staring into the abyss.

I do not know how long...
I could not count the hours, they ran so fast—
Like little bare-foot urchins—shaking my hands away.

But I remember
Somewhere water trickled like a thin severed vein
And a wind came out of the grass,
Touching me gently, tentatively, like a paw.

As the night grew
The gray cloud that had covered the sky like sackcloth
Fell in ashen folds about the hills,
Like hooded virgins pulling their cloaks about them...
There must have been a spent moon,
For the tall one's veil held a shimmer of silver. ...

This too I remember,
And the tenderly rocking mountain,
Silence,
And beating stars. ....

II.

Dawn
Lay like a waxen hand upon the world,
And folded hills
Broke into a solemn wonder of peaks stemming clear and cold,
Till the Tall One bloomed like a lily,
Flecked with sun
Fine as a golden pollen.
It seemed a wind might blow it from the snow.

I smelled the raw sweet essences of things,
And heard spiders in the leaves,
And ticking of little feet
As tiny creatures came out of their doors
To see God pouring light into his star.

It seemed life held
No future and no past for me but this.

And I too got up stiffly from the earth
And held my heart up like a cup.

—Lola Ridge

I Wake You from a Dream of Winter

In your mouth this morning, there
were Manitoba's icy water lanes, when I
kissed it, there were Tundra Swans
passing overhead, like black snow, dense

as swathes of pelts put on for burrowing
deep. Though the season still rushes green
birds bearing coal-dark berries through
the dogwood branches, I will carry

the splintered stars of frost upon my tongue
until you sleep again—I promise—
careful not to close my teeth. Invite me
underneath the blanket of their passage

—cygnet, cob, the Mute, the Trumpeter.
I would leave the ordinary offices of day.

Husband me into night migration.
Teach me navigation by the stars

and where the reed beds thicken. I will speak you
back the cold returning, ecstatic as the arctic air.

—Anne M. Doe Overstreet

Wood Song

I heard a wood thrush in the dusk
　　Twirl three notes and make a star—
My heart that walked with bitterness
　　Came back from very far.

Three shining notes were all he had,
　　And yet they made a starry call—
I caught life back against my breast
　　And kissed it, scars and all.

—Sara Teasdale

When I Heard the Learn'd Astronomer

When I heard the learn'd astronomer,
When the proofs, the figures, were ranged in columns before me,
When I was shown the charts and diagrams, to add, divide, and
    measure them,
When I sitting heard the astronomer where he lectured with much
    applause in the lecture-room,
How soon unaccountable I became tired and sick,
Till rising and gliding out I wander'd off by myself,
In the mystical moist night-air, and from time to time,
Look'd up in perfect silence at the stars.

—Walt Whitman

The Migration of Darkness *excerpt*

Each evening, shortly after sunset,
darkness covers the land.
    Having mystified thinkers for millennia,
    the mechanism for this occurrence
    has now been identified: migration.
Darkness, it has been found, is composed
of an almost infinite number of particles,
which roost and reproduce up north
where they have fewer natural enemies:
    Forest fires, lampposts, lasers, blazing sunlight,
    torches, candles, lighthouses, limelight, and electricity
    are relatively rare in the polar regions.

—Peter Payack

"Leave this chanting and singing and telling of beads!"

Leave this chanting and singing and telling of beads! Whom dost thou worship in this lonely dark corner of a temple with doors all shut? Open thine eyes and see thy God is not before thee!

He is there where the tiller is tilling the hard ground and where the pathmaker is breaking stones. He is with them in sun and in shower, and his garment is covered with dust. Put off thy holy mantle and even like him come down on the dusty soil!

Deliverance? Where is this deliverance to be found? Our master himself has joyfully taken upon him the bonds of creation; he is bound with us all for ever.

Come out of thy meditations and leave aside thy flowers and incense! What harm is there if thy clothes become tattered and stained? Meet him and stand by him in toil and in sweat of thy brow.

—Rabindranath Tagore

Shapeshifting

When young Dawn with her rose-red fingers shone once more...

—Homer

Give the night back to the night,
the stars back to the sky—
Give the earth, spinning in space,
back to the earth—

                    (the stars look black tonight)

Give the moon, no, keep the moon,
it is the stars we want to give back—

Give the soil back to the isopod
emerging to the surface

(what is it looking for?)

Give the Dawn back her rose-red fingers,
she needs them more than the night.

Give the bluejay back his morning,
taken from him by the chickadee—

(sounds are deeper in solitude)

Give back to the sunshine
what darkness is his—

Give back to the night
what light is hers—

(stars, moon, clouds—)

Shape-shifting: bluejay into chickadee
into bluejay, night into day

into—what?

("harassed unrest"?)

Give back to the earth what is hers,
she will forgive you for taking it

or she will turn into a wolf.

—Scott Edward Anderson

Spelt from Sibyl's Leaves

Earnest, earthless, equal, attuneable, | vaulty, voluminous,. .
   stupendous
Evening strains to be tíme's vást, | womb-of-all, home-of-all,
   hearse-of-all night.
Her fond yellow hornlight wound to the west, | her wild hollow
   hoarlight hung to the height
Waste; her earliest stars, earl-stars, | stárs principal, overbend us,
Fíre-féaturing heaven. For earth | her being has unbound; her
   dapple is at an end, as-
tray or aswarm, all throughther, in throngs; | self ín self steepèd
   and páshed—qúite
Disremembering, dísmémbering, | áll now. Heart, you round
   me right
With: Óur évening is over us; óur night | whélms, whélms, ánd
   will end us.
Only the beak-leaved boughs dragonish | damask the tool-smooth
   bleak light; black,
Ever so black on it. Óur tale, O óur oracle! | Lét life, wáned, ah lét
   life wind
Off hér once skéined stained véined varíety | upon, áll on twó
   spools; párt, pen, páck
Now her áll in twó flocks, twó folds—black, white; | right, wrong;
   reckon but, reck but, mind
But thése two; wáre of a wórld where bút these | twó tell, each
   off the óther; of a rack
Where, selfwrung, selfstrung, sheathe-and shelterless, | thóughts
   agaínst thoughts ín groans grínd.

—Gerard Manley Hopkins

Redbirds

Redbirds, redbirds,
  Long and long ago,
What a honey-call you had
  In hills I used to know;

Redbud, buckberry,
  Wild plum-tree
And proud river sweeping
  Southward to the sea,

Brown and gold in the sun
  Sparkling far below,
Trailing stately round her bluffs
  Where the poplars grow—

Redbirds, redbirds,
  Are you singing still
As you sang one May day
  On Saxton's Hill?

—Sara Teasdale

Nutting

　　　　—It seems a day
(I speak of one from many singled out)
One of those heavenly days that cannot die;
When, in the eagerness of boyish hope,
I left our cottage-threshold, sallying forth
With a huge wallet o'er my shoulders slung,
A nutting-crook in hand; and turned my steps
Tow'rd some far-distant wood, a Figure quaint,
Tricked out in proud disguise of cast-off weeds
Which for that service had been husbanded,
By exhortation of my frugal Dame—
Motley accoutrement, of power to smile
At thorns, and brakes, and brambles,—and, in truth,
More ragged than need was! O'er pathless rocks,
Through beds of matted fern, and tangled thickets,
Forcing my way, I came to one dear nook
Unvisited, where not a broken bough
Drooped with its withered leaves, ungracious sign
Of devastation; but the hazels rose
Tall and erect, with tempting clusters hung,
A virgin scene!—A little while I stood,
Breathing with such suppression of the heart
As joy delights in; and, with wise restraint
Voluptuous, fearless of a rival, eyed
The banquet;—or beneath the trees I sate
Among the flowers, and with the flowers I played;
A temper known to those, who, after long
And weary expectation, have been blest
With sudden happiness beyond all hope.
Perhaps it was a bower beneath whose leaves

The violets of five seasons re-appear
And fade, unseen by any human eye;
Where fairy water-breaks do murmur on
For ever; and I saw the sparkling foam,
And—with my cheek on one of those green stones
That, fleeced with moss, under the shady trees,
Lay round me, scattered like a flock of sheep—
I heard the murmur, and the murmuring sound,
In that sweet mood when pleasure loves to pay
Tribute to ease; and, of its joy secure,
The heart luxuriates with indifferent things,
Wasting its kindliness on stocks and stones,
And on the vacant air. Then up I rose,
And dragged to earth both branch and bough, with crash
And merciless ravage: and the shady nook
Of hazels, and the green and mossy bower,
Deformed and sullied, patiently gave up
Their quiet being: and, unless I now
Confound my present feelings with the past;
Ere from the mutilated bower I turned
Exulting, rich beyond the wealth of kings,
I felt a sense of pain when I beheld
The silent trees, and saw the intruding sky.—
Then, dearest Maiden, move along these shades
In gentleness of heart; with gentle hand
Touch—for there is a spirit in the woods.

—William Wordsworth

Sorrow Gondola No. 2

I

Two old men, father-and son-in-law, Liszt and Wagner, are staying
    by the Grand Canal
together with the restless woman who is married to King Midas,
he who changes everything he touches to Wagner.
The ocean's green cold pushes up through the palazzo floors.
Wagner is marked, his famous Punchinello profile looks more tired
    than before,
his face a white flag.
The gondola is heavy-laden with their lives, two round trips
    and a one-way.

II

A window in the palazzo flies open and everyone grimaces in
    the sudden draft.
Outside on the water the trash gondola appears, paddled by two
    one-oared bandits.
Liszt has written down some chords so heavy, they ought
    to be sent off
to the mineralogical institute in Padua for analysis.
Meteorites!
Too heavy to rest, they can only sink and sink straight through the
    future all the way down to the Brownshirt years.
The gondola is heavy-laden with the future's huddled-up stones.

III

Peep-holes into 1990.

March 25th. Angst for Lithuania.

Dreamt I visited a large hospital.
No personnel. Everyone was a patient.

In the same dream a newborn girl
who spoke in complete sentences.

IV

Beside the son-in-law, who's a man of the times, Liszt is a moth-
    eaten grand seigneur.
It's a disguise.
The deep, that tries on and rejects different masks, has chosen this
    one just for him—
the deep that wants to enter people without ever showing its face.

V

Abbé Liszt is used to carrying his suitcase himself through sleet
    and sunshine
and when his time comes to die, there will be no one to meet him
    at the station.
A mild breeze of gifted cognac carries him away in the midst
    of a commission.
He always has commissions.
Two thousand letters a year!
The schoolboy who writes his misspelled word a hundred times
    before he's allowed to go home.
The gondola is heavy-laden with life, it is simple and black.

VI

Back to 1990.

Dreamt I drove over a hundred miles in vain.
Then everything magnified. Sparrows as big as hens
sang so loud that it briefly struck me deaf.

Dreamt I had drawn piano keys
on my kitchen table. I played on them, mute.
The neighbors came over to listen.

VII

The clavier, which kept silent through all of Parsifal (but listened),
    finally has something to say.
Sighs...*sospiri*...
When Liszt plays tonight he holds the sea-pedal pressed down
so the ocean's green force rises up through the floor and flows
    together with all the stone in the building.
Good evening, beautiful deep!
The gondola is heavy-laden with life, it is simple and black.

VIII

Dreamt I was supposed to start school but arrived too late.
Everyone in the room was wearing a white mask.
Whoever the teacher was, no one could say.

—Tomas Tranströmer

The Indigo Glass in the Grass

Which is real—
This bottle of indigo glass in the grass,
Or the bench with the pot of geraniums, the stained mattress and
    the washed overalls drying in the sun?
Which of these truly contains the world?

Neither one, nor the two together.

—Wallace Stevens

River Song

Swift and silent and strong
    Under the low-browed arches,
Through culverts, and under bridges,
Sweeping with long forced marches
Down to the ultimate ridges,—
    The sand, and the reeds, and the midges,
And the down-dropping tassels of larches,
    That border the ocean of song.

    Swift and silent and deep
    Through the noisome and smoke-grimed city,
Turning the wheels and the spindles,
    And the great looms that have no pity,—
Weight, and pulley, and windlass,
    And steel that flashes and kindles,

And hears no forest-learnt ditty,
    Not even in dreams and sleep.

    Blithe and merry and sweet
    Over its shallows singing,—
I hear before I awaken
    The Bound of the church-bells ringing,
And the sound of the leaves wind-shaken,
    Complaining and sun-forsaken,
And the oriole warbling and singing,
    And the swish of the wind in the wheat

    Sweet and tender and true!
    From meadows of blossoming clover,
Where sleepy-eyed cows are lowing,
    And bobolinks twittering over,—
Ebbing and falling and flowing—
    Singing and gliding and going—
The river—my silver-shod lover,
    Down to the infinite blue.

    Deep, and tender, and strong!
    With resonant voice and hole—
To far away sunshiny places,
    Haunts of the bee and the swallow,
Where the Sabbath is sweet with the praises
    Of dumb things, of weeds and of daisies,—
Oh river! I hear thee—I follow
    To the ocean where I too belong.

—Kate Seymour Maclean

Lights

When we come home at night and close the door,
 Standing together in the shadowy room,
 Safe in our own love and the gentle gloom,
Glad of familiar wall and chair and floor,

Glad to leave far below the clanging city;
 Looking far downward to the glaring street
 Gaudy with light, yet tired with many feet,
In both of us wells up a wordless pity;

Men have tried hard to put away the dark;
 A million lighted windows brilliantly
  Inlay with squares of gold the winter night,
But to us standing here there comes the stark
  Sense of the lives behind each yellow light,
 And not one wholly joyous, proud, or free.

—Sara Teasdale

Home and the Homeless

The buildings are worn.
The trees are strong and ancient.
They bend against the grid of electric lines.
The windows are broken
by the homeless and the cold past.
I am home on the yard
that spreads mint, pales the Victorian roses,
takes into it the ravaged lilac tree.
The black bulk of plastic lies about
stopping unwanted weeds for the Landlord.
Tattered, the cedar tree is chipped to dry heaps of recklessness.
The unwanted spreads by the power of neglect.
The wear of traffic says that we are out of time,
must hurry.

Age, the creak in the handmade screen door fades behind itself.

—Elizabeth Woody

The Oak Desk

—for Adeline Woodward Baker

Her elbow rested here
a century ago.
This is the field

she looked out on,
a mad rush of wheat
anchored to the barn.

What her thoughts were,
the words she penned
are driven into the grain,

its deep tide crossing
under my hand. She breathes
through the knothole.

Outside, the wind
pushes the farm
down an alley of stars.

—Wyatt Townley

Do not stand at my grave and weep

Do not stand at my grave and weep.
I am not there. I do not sleep.
I am a thousand winds that blow.
I am the diamond glints on snow.

I am the sunlight on ripened grain.
I am the gentle autumn rain.
When you awaken in the morning's hush
I am the swift uplifting rush

Of quiet birds in circled flight.
I am the soft stars that shine at night.
Do not stand at my grave and cry;
I am not there. I did not die.

—Mary Elizabeth Frye

On the Dunes

If there is any life when death is over,
    These tawny beaches will know much of me,
I shall come back, as constant and as changeful
    As the unchanging, many-colored sea.

If life was small, if it has made me scornful,
    Forgive me; I shall straighten like a flame
In the great calm of death, and if you want me
    Stand on the sea-ward dunes and call my name.

—Sara Teasdale

The Chesapeake & Ohio Canal

Thick now with the sludge from the years of suburbs, with toys,
fenders, wine bottles, tampons, skeletons of possums, and
edged by blankets of leaves, jellied wrappers unshakably
stuck to the scrub pines that somehow lift themselves
from the mossed wall of blockstone headlined a hundred
years back, this water is bruised as a shoe at Goodwill.
Its brown goes nowhere, neither does it remain, and elms
bend over its heavy back like patient fans, dreamlessly.
This is the death of hope's commerce, the death of cities
blank as winter light, the death of people who are gone
erratic and hopeless as summer's glittering water-skimmers.
Yet the two climbing that path like a single draft horse
saw the heart of the water break open only minutes ago,
and the rainbow trout walked its tail as if the evening
arranged an offering in an unimaginable room where plans
inched ahead for the people, as if the trout always meant
to hang from that chain, to be borne through the last shades
like a lure sent carefully, deviously in the blue ache of
air thickening in still streets and between brown walls.

—Dave Smith

I Was Sleeping Where the Black Oaks Move

We watched from the house
as the river grew, helpless
and terrible in its unfamiliar body.
Wrestling everything into it,
the water wrapped around trees
until their life-hold was broken.
They went down, one by one,
and the river dragged off their covering.

Nests of the herons, roots washed to bones,
snags of soaked bark on the shoreline:
a whole forest pulled through the teeth
of the spillway. Trees surfacing
singly, where the river poured off
into arteries for fields below the reservation.

When at last it was over, the long removal,
they had all become the same dry wood.
We walked among them, the branches
whitening in the raw sun.
Above us drifted herons,
alone, hoarse-voiced, broken,
settling their beaks among the hollows.
Grandpa said, *These are the ghosts of the tree people*
moving among us, unable to take their rest.

Sometimes now, we dream our way back to the heron dance.
Their long wings are bending the air
into circles through which they fall.
They rise again in shifting wheels.

How long must we live in the broken figures
their necks make, narrowing the sky.

—Louise Erdrich

Shadow Questions

(for Shadow)

How can so small a body
cast such a long shadow

how can the shadow stay with us
without the body

how can so quiet a creature
still greet us after the paws have gone

—W. S. Merwin

How to Be a Poet

(to remind myself)

Make a place to sit down.
Sit down. Be quiet.
You must depend upon
affection, reading, knowledge,

skill—more of each
than you have—inspiration,
work, growing older, patience,
for patience joins time
to eternity. Any readers
who like your work,
doubt their judgment.

Breathe with unconditional breath
the unconditioned air.
Shun electric wire.
Communicate slowly. Live
a three-dimensioned life;
stay away from screens.
Stay away from anything
that obscures the place it is in.
There are no unsacred places;
there are only sacred places
and desecrated places.

Accept what comes from silence.
Make the best you can of it.
Of the little words that come
out of the silence, like prayers
prayed back to the one who prays,
make a poem that does not disturb
the silence from which it came.

—Wendell Berry

North Dakota

east

the whole moon
burns behind jamestown

seven wings of geese
light the thin ice

west

the asian sun
bloody on the interstate

spring flowers
break on the gray prairie

exit

fingerprints
on the rearview mirror

feral shadows
transposed near fargo

—Gerald Vizenor

But You Thought You Knew What a Sign Looked Like

Open your hands, lift them.
　　　—William Stafford, "Today"

The parking space beside the store when you
were late. The man who showed up just in time
to hold the door when you were juggling five
big packages. The spider plant that grew—
though you forgot to water it. The new
nest in the tree outside your window. Chime
of distant church bells when you're lonely. Rhyme
of friendship. Apples. Sky a trove of blue.

And who's to say these miracles are less
significant than burning bushes, loaves
and fishes, steps on water. We are blessed
by marvels wearing ordinary clothes—
how easily we're fooled by simple dress—
Oranges. Water. Leaves. Bread. Crows.

—Rosemerry Wahtola Trommer

The Darkling Thrush

I leant upon a coppice gate
　　When Frost was spectre-gray,
And Winter's dregs made desolate
　　The weakening eye of day.
The tangled bine-stems scored the sky

Like strings of broken lyres,
And all mankind that haunted nigh
    Had sought their household fires.

The land's sharp features seemed to be
    The Century's corpse outleant,
His crypt the cloudy canopy,
    The wind his death-lament.
The ancient pulse of germ and birth
    Was shrunken hard and dry,
And every spirit upon earth
    Seemed fervourless as I.

At once a voice arose among
    The bleak twigs overhead
In a full-hearted evensong
    Of joy illimited;
An aged thrush, frail, gaunt, and small,
    In blast-beruffled plume,
Had chosen thus to fling his soul
    Upon the growing gloom.

So little cause for carolings
    Of such ecstatic sound
Was written on terrestrial things
    Afar or nigh around,
That I could think there trembled through
    His happy good-night air
Some blessed Hope, whereof he knew
    And I was unaware.

—Thomas Hardy

To the Cuckoo

O blithe New-comer! I have heard,
I hear thee and rejoice.
O Cuckoo! shall I call thee Bird,
Or but a wandering Voice?

While I am lying on the grass
Thy twofold shout I hear;
From hill to hill it seems to pass,
At once far off, and near.

Though babbling only to the Vale
Of sunshine and of flowers,
Thou bringest unto me a tale
Of visionary hours.

Thrice welcome, darling of the Spring!
Even yet thou art to me
No bird, but an invisible thing,
A voice, a mystery;

The same whom in my school-boy days
I listened to; that Cry
Which made me look a thousand ways
In bush, and tree, and sky.

To seek thee did I often rove
Through woods and on the green;
And thou wert still a hope, a love;
Still longed for, never seen.

And I can listen to thee yet;
Can lie upon the plain

And listen, till I do beget
That golden time again.

O blessèd Bird! the earth we pace
Again appears to be
An unsubstantial, faery place;
That is fit home for Thee!

—William Wordsworth

"A narrow Fellow in the Grass"

A narrow Fellow in the Grass
Occasionally rides –
You may have met him? Did you not
His notice instant is –

The Grass divides as with a Comb,
A spotted Shaft is seen,
And then it closes at your Feet
And opens further on –

He likes a Boggy Acre –
A Floor too cool for Corn –
But when a Boy and Barefoot
I more than once at Noon

Have passed I thought a Whip Lash
Unbraiding in the Sun
When stooping to secure it
It wrinkled And was gone –

Several of Nature's People
I know, and they know me
I feel for them a transport
Of Cordiality

But never met this Fellow
Attended or alone
Without a tighter Breathing
And Zero at the Bone.

—Emily Dickinson

Snake

A snake came to my water-trough
On a hot, hot day, and I in pyjamas for the heat,
To drink there.

In the deep, strange-scented shade of the great dark carob-tree
I came down the steps with my pitcher
And must wait, must stand and wait, for there he was at the trough
    before me.

He reached down from a fissure in the earth-wall in the gloom
And trailed his yellow-brown slackness soft-bellied down, over the
    edge of the stone trough
And rested his throat upon the stone bottom,
And where the water had dripped from the tap, in a small
    clearness,
He sipped with his straight mouth,

Softly drank through his straight gums, into his slack long body,
Silently.

Someone was before me at my water-trough,
And I, like a second-comer, waiting.

He lifted his head from his drinking, as cattle do,
And looked at me vaguely, as drinking cattle do,
And flickered his two-forked tongue from his lips, and mused
  a moment,
And stooped and drank a little more,
Being earth-brown, earth-golden from the burning bowels of
  the earth
On the day of Sicilian July, with Etna smoking.

The voice of my education said to me
He must be killed,
For in Sicily the black, black snakes are innocent, the gold are
  venomous.

And voices in me said, If you were a man
You would take a stick and break him now, and finish him off.

But must I confess how I liked him,
How glad I was he had come like a guest in quiet, to drink at
  my water-trough
And depart peaceful, pacified, and thankless,
Into the burning bowels of this earth?

Was it cowardice, that I dared not kill him?
Was it perversity, that I longed to talk to him?
Was it humility, to feel so honoured?
I felt so honoured.

And yet those voices:
If you were not afraid, you would kill him!

And truly I was afraid, I was most afraid,
But even so, honoured still more
That he should seek my hospitality
From out the dark door of the secret earth.

He drank enough
And lifted his head, dreamily, as one who has drunken,
And flickered his tongue like a forked night on the air, so black,
Seeming to lick his lips,
And looked around like a god, unseeing, into the air,
And slowly turned his head,
And slowly, very slowly, as if thrice adream,
Proceeded to draw his slow length curving round
And climb again the broken bank of my wall-face.

And as he put his head into that dreadful hole,
And as he slowly drew up, snake-easing his shoulders, and entered
    farther,
A sort of horror, a sort of protest against his withdrawing into
    that horrid black hole,
Deliberately going into the blackness, and slowly drawing himself
    after,
Overcame me now his back was turned.

I looked round, I put down my pitcher,
I picked up a clumsy log
And threw it at the water-trough with a clatter.
I think it did not hit him,
But suddenly that part of him that was left behind convulsed in
    undignified haste,

Writhed like lightning, and was gone
Into the black hole, the earth-lipped fissure in the wall-front,
At which, in the intense still noon, I stared with fascination.

And immediately I regretted it.
I thought how paltry, how vulgar, what a mean act!
I despised myself and the voices of my accursed human education.

And I thought of the albatross,
And I wished he would come back, my snake.

For he seemed to me again like a king,
Like a king in exile, uncrowned in the underworld,
Now due to be crowned again.

And so, I missed my chance with one of the lords
Of life.
And I have something to expiate;
A pettiness.

                                        Taormina

—D. H. Lawrence

On the Grasshopper and Cricket

The Poetry of earth is never dead:
 When all the birds are faint with the hot sun,
 And hide in cooling trees, a voice will run
From hedge to hedge about the new-mown mead;
That is the Grasshopper's—he takes the lead
 In summer luxury,—he has never done
 With his delights; for when tired out with fun
He rests at ease beneath some pleasant weed.
The poetry of earth is ceasing never:
 On a lone winter evening, when the frost
  Has wrought a silence, from the stove there shrills
The Cricket's song, in warmth increasing ever,
 And seems to one in drowsiness half lost,
  The Grasshopper's among some grassy hills.

—John Keats

Pastoral

Something in the field is
working away. Root-noise.
Twig-noise. Plant
of weak chlorophyll, no
name for it. Something
in the field has mastered
distance by living too close
to fences. Yellow fruit, has it
pit or seeds? Stalk of wither. Grass-
noise fighting weed-noise. Dirt
and chant. Something in the
field. Coreopsis. I did not mean
to say that. Yellow petal, has it
wither-gift? Has it gorgeous
rash? Leaf-loss and worried
sprout, its bursting art. Some-
thing in the. Field fallowed and
cicada. I did not mean to
say. Has it roar and bloom?
Has it road and follow? A thistle
prick, fraught burrs, such
easy attachment. Stem-
and stamen-noise. Can I lime-
flower? Can I chamomile?
Something in the field cannot.

—Jennifer Chang

To a Mouse, On Turning Her up in Her Nest with the Plough, November 1785

Wee, sleekit, cow'rin, tim'rous beastie,
O, what a panic's in thy breastie!
Thou need na start awa sae hasty,
                    Wi' bickering brattle!
I wad be laith to rin an' chase thee,
                    Wi' murd'ring pattle!

I'm truly sorry Man's dominion,
Has broken Nature's social union,
An' justifies that ill opinion,
                    Which makes thee startle,
At me, thy poor, earth-born companion,
                    An' fellow-mortal!

I doubt na, whiles, but thou may thieve;
What then? poor beastie, thou maun live!
A daimen-icker in a thrave
                    'S a sma' request:
I'll get a blessin wi' the lave,
                    An' never miss't!

Thy wee bit housie, too, in ruin!
It's silly wa's the win's are strewin!
An' naething, now, to big a new ane,
                    O' foggage green!
An' bleak December's winds ensuin,
                    Baith snell an' keen!

Thou saw the fields laid bare an' wast,

An' weary winter comin fast,
An' cozie here, beneath the blast,
       Thou thought to dwell—
Till crash! the cruel coulter past
       Out thro' thy cell.

That wee bit heap o' leaves an' stibble,
Has cost thee mony a weary nibble!
Now thou's turn'd out, for a' thy trouble,
       But house or hald,
To thole the winter's sleety dribble,
       An' cranreuch cauld!

But, Mousie, thou art no thy-lane,
In proving foresight may be vain;
The best-laid schemes o' mice an' men
       Gang aft a-gley,
An' le'e us nought but grief an' pain,
       For promis'd joy!

Still thou art blest, compar'd wi' me
The present only toucheth thee:
But och! I backward cast my e'e.
       On prospects drear!
An' forward, tho' I canna see,
       I guess an' fear!

—Robert Burns

Today, When I Could Do Nothing

Today, when I could do nothing,
I saved an ant.

It must have come in with the morning paper,
still being delivered
to those who shelter in place.

A morning paper is still an essential service.

I am not an essential service.

I have coffee and books,
time,
a garden,
silence enough to fill cisterns.

It must have first walked
the morning paper, as if loosened ink
taking the shape of an ant.

Then across the laptop computer—warm—
then onto the back of a cushion.

Small black ant, alone,
crossing a navy cushion,
moving steadily because that is what it could do.

Set outside in the sun,
it could not have found again its nest.
What then did I save?
It did not move as if it was frightened,
even while walking my hand,
which moved it through swiftness and air.

Ant, alone, without companions,
whose ant-heart I could not fathom—
how is your life, I wanted to ask.

I lifted it, took it outside.

This first day when I could do nothing,
contribute nothing
beyond staying distant from my own kind,
I did this.

—Jane Hirshfield

Haiku Journey

i. Spring

the tips of each pine
the spikes of telephone poles
hold gathering crows

may's errant mustard
spreads wild across paved road
look both ways

roadside treble cleft
feeding gopher, paws to mouth
cheeks puffed with music

yesterday's spring wind
ruffling the grey tips of fur
rabbit dandelion

ii. Summer

turkey vulture feeds
mechanical as a red oil rig
head rocks down up down

stiff-legged dog rises
goes grumbling after squirrel
old ears still flap

snowy egret—curves,
lines, sculpted against pond blue;
white clouds against sky

banded headed bird
this ballerina killdeer
dance on point my heart

iii. Fall

leaf wind cold through coat
wails over hills, through barren trees
empty garbage cans dance

damp September night
lone farmer, lighted tractor
drive memory's worn path

sky black with migration
flocks settle on barren trees
leaf birds, travel songs

october moon cast
over corn, lighted fields
crinkled sheaves of white

iv. Winter

ground painted in frost
thirsty morning sun drinks white
leaves rust golds return

winter bare branches
hold tattered cups of summer
empty nests trail twigs

lace edges of ice
manna against darkened sky
words turn with weather

now one to seven
deer or haiku syllables
weave through winter trees

Northern follows jig
body flashes with strike, dive:
broken line floats up.

—Kimberly Blaeser

Passing Through Seongeup Village

Whenever I gaze into a horse's virtuous eyes, it seems to
know nothing but the indigent evening in the direction
the wind is blowing from.

—Lee Si-Young

Elm in Dirt with Bird

Shivering, stubborn, confused,
the hummingbird clung to her nest,

marooned in her tiny lifeboat
of down and spider silk.

In a pruning fury,
I had cut her out of the sky,

leaving branch, nest, and shark-tooth saw
symbolically on the ground

like some kind of protest art:
Elm in Dirt with Bird.

Her eyes followed me
as I comically tied her severed foothold,

home to her sole creation and possession,
back inside the green fountain of foliage.

The ancient surge of April
trembled in her wings,

waiting for Death to lower its head,
waiting for the world to begin again.

—Jack Cooper

Flood

We drive the car into the next morning,
over a distance we're happy
to lose sight of. Memory rises with the river,
and brown water fills the fields,
turned to stubble in this cold.
The arc of the bridge is too high to look back.
The river rises and drives us, the forced sing along,
your foot heavy on the gas pedal.
There were no stars last night. I pass time
rummaging through what we chose to take:
this story, a few battered pots and pans,
one lamp—its aqua shade turned up.

Everything will disappear into this thick water,
into last night when we told each other
what we had kept secret for years.
It's dangerous to dream along, to ignore
natural disaster. We point the car
toward the horizon, wanting to be a point
on its line, a place of motion, nothing more.

—Janet McAdams

Gathering Leaves

Spades take up leaves
No better than spoons,
And bags full of leaves
Are light as balloons.

I make a great noise
Of rustling all day
Like rabbit and deer
Running away.

But the mountains I raise
Elude my embrace,
Flowing over my arms
And into my face.

I may load and unload
Again and again
Till I fill the whole shed,
And what have I then?

Next to nothing for weight;
And since they grew duller
From contact with earth,
Next to nothing for color.

Next to nothing for use,
But a crop is a crop,
And who's to say where
The harvest shall stop?

—Robert Frost

Sonnet VI

A pine tree in your right hand. A willow in your left. This
is summer: one of your hundred gazelles has surrendered to the dew
and slept on my shoulder, near one of your regions, and what
if the wolf notices, and a forest burns in the distance

Your sleepiness is stronger than fear. A wilderness of your beauty
dozes off, and a moon out of your shadows wakes to guard its trees.
What's the name of the place your footsteps tattooed on the ground
a heavenly ground for the salaam of the birds, near echo?

And stronger than the sword is your sleep between your
    streamlined arms,
like two rivers, in the dreamer's paradise, of what you do on the banks
to yourself carried above yourself. The wolf might carry a flute
and cry by the river: What isn't feminized...is in vain

A bit of weakness in metaphor is enough for tomorrow
for the berries to ripen on the fence, and for the sword to break
    beneath the dew

—Mahmoud Darwish

When Morning Comes

I open my mouth and breathe the day,
wish for a kiss like the one this golden trumpet
of jewelweed is getting full on the lips.
Furry bumblebee embraces her

like there's no tomorrow. And I remember
to hold the moment because it's true, there may not be
a morning after. And this is why I pause when
rusty shovel unearths rotted pit, peach long gone,

her hope for progeny emptied, but home
to red ants now, tiny thousands pouring forth like honey,
spilling onto cocoa shells newly lain beneath the hyssop,
soft pink and pungent. Now I trouble

the bronze-suited honeybee who is fumbling
Russian Sage, tickling her purply-blue tongues, riding her
shining silver leaves that curl in rainbowed mist.
Shall I forget the three-leafed maple fragment

red upon the stair, its green seeds like outstretched arms
now blushing dusty rose. Let me not forget these seeds,
nor the catbird who delights to echo each whine
of my clipping shears, nor the Bible Leaf

relieved of yellow flower but fragrant still
when I break a spear and press it to my face. Let me
not forget the white carnation, purple aster, and the stars
who shut their eyes and sleep when morning comes.

—L. L. Barkat

"The morning sea of silence broke into ripples of bird songs"

The morning sea of silence broke into ripples of bird songs; and the flowers were all merry by the roadside; and the wealth of gold was scattered through the rift of the clouds while we busily went on our way and paid no heed.

We sang no glad songs nor played; we went not to the village for barter; we spoke not a word nor smiled; we lingered not on the way. We quickened our pace more and more as the time sped by.

The sun rose to the mid sky and doves cooed in the shade. Withered leaves danced and whirled in the hot air of noon. The shepherd boy drowsed and dreamed in the shadow of the banyan tree, and I laid myself down by the water and stretched my tired limbs on the grass.

My companions laughed at me in scorn; they held their heads high and hurried on; they never looked back nor rested; they vanished in the distant blue haze. They crossed many meadows and hills, and passed through strange, far-away countries. All honour to you, heroic host of the interminable path! Mockery and reproach pricked me to rise, but found no response in me. I gave myself up for lost in the depth of a glad humiliation — in the shadow of a dim delight.

The repose of the sun-embroidered green gloom slowly spread over my heart. I forgot for what I had travelled, and I surrendered my mind without struggle to the maze of shadows and songs.

At last, when I woke from my slumber and opened my eyes, I saw thee standing by me, flooding my sleep with thy smile. How I had feared that the path was long and wearisome, and the struggle to reach thee was hard!

—Rabindranath Tagore

Permissions

Anderson, Scott Edward. "Midnight Sun" and "Shapeshifting," from *Fallow Field,* Aldrich Press, 2013. Used by permission of the poet.

Apache, Crisosto. "Carrizo," appeared in *Poetry* magazine, The Poetry Foundation, 2018. Used by permission of the poet.

Barkat, L. L. "On Meeting an Old German Woman by the Hudson River," appeared in *Every Day Poems*, 2021. Used by permission of the poet.

Barkat, L. L. "Return to Sloansville," "Scent," and "When Morning Comes," from *InsideOut: Poems,* International Arts Movement, 2009. Used by permission of the poet.

Barkat, Sara. "Dreaming Backwards." Used by permission of the poet.

Berry, Wendell. "Before Dark" and "The Peace of Wild Things," copyright © 2012 by Wendell Berry, from *New Collected Poems*. Reprinted by permission of Counterpoint Press.

Berry, Wendell. "How to Be a Poet," copyright © 1998 by Wendell Berry, from *The Selected Poems of Wendell Berry*. Reprinted by permission of Counterpoint Press.

Blaeser, Kimberly. "Haiku Journey," from *Apprenticed to Justice*, Salt Publishing, 2007. Used by permission of the poet.

Blake, William. "The Garden of Love," from *Songs of Innocence and of Experience Shewing the Two Contrary States of the Human Soul,* 1794. Public domain.

Burns, Robert. "To a Mouse, On Turning Her up in Her Nest with the Plough, November, 1785," 1785. Public domain.

Burns, Robert. "Verses On The Destruction Of The Woods Near Drumlanrig," 1791. Public domain.

Chang, Jennifer. "Pastoral," originally published in the *New England Review.* Reprinted with permission from *The History of Anonymity* by Jennifer Chang (University of Georgia Press, 2008).

Cob, Briceida Cuevas. "The Owl," translated by Earl Shorris and

Sylvia Sasson Shorris. Published in *Words Without Borders*, September 2005. Translation © 2005 by Earl Shorris and Silvia Sasson Shorris. Used by permission of *Words Without Borders*. All rights reserved.

Cooper, Jack. "Elm in Dirt with Bird," from *Across My Silence*, World Audience Publishers, 2015. Used by permission of the poet.

Darwish, Mahmoud. "The Cypress Broke," "If You Return Alone," "Sonnet VI," from *The Butterfly's Burden,* translated by Fady Joudah. Copyright © 2007 by Mahmoud Darwish. Translation copyright © 2007 by Fady Joudah. Reprinted with the permission of The Permissions Company, LLC on behalf of Copper Canyon Press, coppercanyonpress.org

Dickinson, Emily. "A narrow Fellow in the Grass," from THE POEMS OF EMILY DICKINSON: VARIORUM EDITION, edited by Ralph W. Franklin, Cambridge, Mass.: The Belknap Press of Harvard University Press, Copyright © 1998 by the President and Fellows of Harvard College. Copyright © 1951, 1955 by the President and Fellows of Harvard College. Copyright © renewed 1979, 1983 by the President and Fellows of Harvard College. Copyright © 1914, 1918, 1919, 1924, 1929, 1930, 1932, 1935, 1937, 1942 by Martha Dickinson Bianchi. Copyright © 1952, 1957, 1958, 1963, 1965 by Mary L. Hampson. Used by permission. All rights reserved.

Erdrich, Louise. "I Was Sleeping Where the Black Oaks Move," from *Original Fire* by Louise Erdrich. Copyright © 2003 by Louise Erdrich. Used by permission of HarperCollins Publishers.

Farrokhzad, Forugh. "I Pity the Garden," translated by Sholeh Wolpé. Published in *Words Without Borders*, May 2004. Translation © 2004 by Sholeh Wolpé. Used by permission of *Words Without Borders*. All rights reserved.

Foerster, Jennifer Elise. "Leaving Tulsa," from *Leaving Tulsa* by Jennifer Elise Foerster. © 2013 Jennifer Elise Foerster. Reprinted by permission of The University of Arizona Press.

Frost, Robert. "Christmas Trees," from *Mountain Interval,* 1916, public domain. "Dust of Snow," public domain. "Gathering Leaves," *New Hampshire,* 1923, public domain. "The Wood-Pile," *North of Boston,* 1914, public domain.

Frye, Mary Elizabeth. "Do not stand at my grave and weep." Public domain.

Greenwald, Martha. "Tornado Warning/JoAnn Fabric & Craft," appeared in *Louisville Review.* Used by permission of the poet.

Grotz, Jennifer. "Late Summer," from *Window Left Open.* Copyright © 2016 by Jennifer Grotz. Reprinted with the permission of The Permissions Company, LLC on behalf of Graywolf Press, Minneapolis, Minnesota, graywolfpress.org.

Hardy, Thomas. "The Darkling Thrush," from *The Graphic,* 29, December 1900. (Originally titled "The Century's End, 1900"). Public domain.

Hirshfield, Jane. "Today, when I could do nothing," © 2020 Jane Hirshifield. First appeared in *The San Francisco Chronicle* https://datebook.sfchronicle.com/books/a-poem-about-finding-life-while-we-shelter-in-place. Used by permission of Jane Hirshfield, all rights reserved.

Hirshfield, Jane. "Tree," © 2001 Jane Hirshfield, from *Given Sugar, Given Salt* (NY: HarperCollins, 2001). Used by permission of Jane Hirshfield, all rights reserved.

Hoagland, Tony. "Jet," from *Donkey Gospel.* Copyright © 1998 by Tony Hoagland. Reprinted with the permission of The Permissions Company, LLC on behalf of Graywolf Press, Minneapolis, Minnesota, graywolfpress.org.

Hopkins, Gerard Manley "God's Grandeur" *The Oxford Book of English Mystical Verse,* 1917, public domain. "Inversnaid," "Binsey Poplars," "Pied Beauty," and "Spelt from Sibyl's Leaves," public domain.

Jackson, Major. "Lost Lake" and "My Awe Is a Weakness," from *Holding Company: Poems,* W. W. Norton & Company, 2012. Used by permission of the poet.

Johnson, Emily Pauline. "Marshlands," from *Flint and Feather: Collected Verse*. 1917. Public domain.

K., P. "A Chair on a Highway on a Rainy Afternoon," translated by P. K. Published in *Words Without Borders*, November 2018. Translation © 2018 by P. K. By permission of *Words Without Borders*. All rights reserved.

Kakabadze, Irakli. "It's been three years," translated by Mary Childs and Lia Shartava. Published in *Words Without Borders*, September 2018. Translation © 2018 by Mary Childs. By permission of *Words Without Borders*. All rights reserved.

Kasischke, Laura. "Fashion Victim," from *Where Now: New and Selected Poems*. Copyright © 2007 by Laura Kasischke. Reprinted with the permission of The Permissions Company, LLC on behalf of Copper Canyon Press, www.coppercanyonpress.org.

Kaus, Jan. "Matsiranna," translated by Adam Cullen. Published in *Words Without Borders*, October 2015. Translation © 2015 by Adam Cullen. By permission of *Words Without Borders*. All rights reserved.

Keats, John. "On the Grasshopper and Cricket." Public domain.

Lawrence, D. H. "Snake." Public domain.

Lee, Li-Young. "Degrees of Blue" from *Book of My Nights*. Copyright © 2001 by Li-Young Lee. Reprinted with the permission of The Permissions Company, LLC on behalf of BOA Editions, Ltd., www.boaeditions.org.

Lee, Si-Young. "Passing Through Seongeup Village," translated by Brother Anthony of Taizé and Yoo Hui-Sok. Published in *Words Without Borders*, June 2011. Translation © 2011 by Brother Anthony of Taizé and Yoo Hui-Sok. By permission of *Words Without Borders*. All rights reserved.

Lleshanaku, Luljeta. "Shadows on the Snow," translated by Shpresa Qatipi and Henry Israeli. Published in *Words Without Borders*, January 2004. Translation © 2004 by Shpresa Qatipi and Henry Israeli. By permission of *Words Without Borders*. All rights reserved.

Maclean, Kate Seymour. "River Song" and "The Sabbath Of The

Woods." Public domain.

Maxson, Richard. "Beefsteak" and "Birds in Home Depot— December." Used by permission of the poet.

McAdams, Janet. "Flood," appeared in *Poetry* magazine, The Poetry Foundation, 1989. Used by permission of the poet.

McKay, Claude. "I Shall Return," from *Harlem Shadows*, Harcourt, Brace and Company, 1922. Public domain.

Merwin, W. S. "Living with the News" and "Shadow Questions," from *W. S. Merwin Selected Poems*, (Bloodaxe Books, 2007). Reproduced with permission of Bloodaxe Books. www.bloodaxebooks.com.

Merwin, W. S. "Living with the News" and "Shadow Questions," from *Garden Time*. Copyright © 2016 by W. S. Merwin. Reprinted with the permission of The Permissions Company, LLC on behalf of Copper Canyon Press, www.coppercanyonpress.org.

Murphy, Sandra Fox. "Jonah's Revenge." Used by permission of the poet.

Neruda, Pablo. "The Egoist," translated by Forrest Gander, from *The Essential Neruda: Selected Poems*, edited by Mark Eisner. Copyright © 2004 by Forrest Gander. Reprinted with the permission of The Permissions Company, LLC on behalf of City Lights Books, citylights.com.

Neruda, Pablo. "El egoista," *Jardín de invierno*. © Pablo Neruda, 1974 and Fundación Pablo Neruda. Reprinted with permission of Fundación Pablo Neruda.

Ortega, Michelle. "Dead River Road," from *Don't Ask Why,* Seven Kitchens Press, 2020. Reprinted by permission of the poet.

Overstreet, Anne M. Doe. "I Wake You from a Dream of Winter," appeared in *Every Day Poems*, May 21, 2013. Used by permission of the poet.

Payack, Peter. "The Migration of Darkness," excerpt, 1980 Rhysling Award for the Best Poem in Science Fiction. Named the number one poem that unites art and science by Quirk Press. Used by permission of the poet.

Ridge, Lola. "The Edge," from *Poetry* magazine, The Poetry Foundation, October 1918. Public domain.

Shang, Hermit Tai. "Reply to People," translated by Jeffrey Yang. Published in *Words Without Borders*, May 2004. Translation © 2004 by Jeffrey Yang. By permission of *Words Without Borders*. All rights reserved.

Smith, Dave. "The Chesapeake & Ohio Canal," appeared in *Poetry* magazine, The Poetry Foundation, September, 1983. Used by permission of the poet.

Stevens, Wallace. "The Indigo Glass in the Grass," from *Poetry* magazine, The Poetry Foundation, 1919. Public domain.

Tagore, Rabindranath. "Leave this chanting and singing and telling of beads!," "On the day when the lotus bloomed, alas, my mind was straying," and "The morning sea of silence broke into ripples of bird songs," from *Gitanjali: Song Offerings,* 1913. Public domain.

Teasdale, Sara. "Lost Things," "Places," "On the Dunes," "Redbirds," "The New Moon," from *Flame and Shadow,* The MacMillan Company, 1920. Public domain. "Lights," "Wood Song," from *Love Songs*, The MacMillan Company, 1917. Public domain.

Townley, Wyatt. "The Oak Desk," from *The Afterlives of Trees.* Woodley Press, 2011. Used by permission of the poet.

Tranströmer, Tomas. "Sorrow Gondola No. 2," translated by Patty Crane, from *Bright Scythe: Selected Poems.* Copyright © 2015 by Tomas Tranströmer. English translation copyright © 2015 by Patty Crane. Reprinted with the permission of The Permissions Company, LLC on behalf of Sarabande Books, www.sarabande books.org.

Trommer, Rosemerry Wahtola. "But You Thought You Knew What a Sign Looked Like," appeared at Gratefulness.org. Used by permission of the poet.

Vizenor, Gerald. "North Dakota," from *Almost Ashore*, Salt, 2006. Used by permission of the poet.

Whitman, Walt. "When I Heard the Learn'd Astronomer," from *McClure's Magazine*, Volume 9, October 1897. Public domain.

Willingham, Will. "Dam," poem shared at Tweetspeakpoetry.com. "In my defense, there was a very dense fog" and "Poetry Slam," first appeared in *Every Day Poems* on December 11, 2013 and October 4, 2013. Reprinted by permission of the poet.

Woody, Elizabeth. "Home and the Homeless," from *Luminaries of the Humble* by Elizabeth Woody. © 1994 Elizabeth Woody. Reprinted by permission of the University of Arizona Press.

Wordsworth, William. "I wandered lonely as a cloud," "Nutting," and "To the Cuckoo." Public domain.

Yeats, William Butler. "The Lake Isle of Innisfree," appeared in *National Observer,* 1890. Public domain.

Also From T. S. Poetry Press

How to Read a Poem: Based on the Billy Collins Poem "Introduction to Poetry," by Tania Runyan

"No reader, experienced or new to reading poems, will want to miss this winsome and surprising way into the rich, wonderful conversations that poetry makes possible."

—David Wright, Assistant Professor of English at Monmouth College, IL

How to Write a Form Poem: A Guided Tour of 10 Fabulous Forms by Tania Runyan, editors Sara Barkat and L.L. Barkat

"An accessible book with clear explanations, sample poems, exercises, and good humor that will appeal to writers of all sorts. If you want to teach students about poetic forms or learn more yourself, then you need to get this book."

—Katie Manning, professor of writing at Point Loma Nazarene University, poetry featured on Krista Tippett's *On Being* program

T. S. Poetry Press titles are available online in e-book and print editions. Print editions also available through Ingram.

tspoetry.com

Made in the USA
Middletown, DE
09 July 2022

68702693R00080